D1345164

Jacqueline Wilson

ILLUSTRATED BY NICK SHARRATT

Diary 2015

DOUBLEDAY

THIS DIARY BELONGS TO:

Name: Melissa Munt

Address: 22 A Little Wothrowd OX33 ltr

Phone number: 0781557924

Email: Munt Melissa@Aol.Com

Birthday: 207 28th march

IN THE SPOTLIGHT!

Have you ever been on stage? You might have been in a school play or talent show; acting, singing, dancing, or playing a musical instrument. Maybe you told jokes, juggled, or performed magic tricks!

Lots of the characters in Jacqueline Wilson's books have performed on stage. Some love being in the spotlight! In *Starring Tracy Beaker*, Tracy can't believe her luck when she's given the lead role in her school play!

In *Little Darlings*, Destiny's year are putting on a talent show, and Destiny shocks them all when she sings beautifully in front of them for the first time. Even Hetty Feather performs on stage, as a mermaid in *Sapphire Battersea*.

She then becomes the ringmaster at Tanglefield's Travelling Circus in *Emerald Star*!

ELSA SAYS: Why not talk to your teacher about putting on a show? Or you could organise your own with some friends! You could make it a competition, or just for fun.

BEHIND THE SCENES!

Some people really don't like to be the centre of attention, of course! In *Double Act*, Ruby is desperate to be an actress, but her twin Garnet would much rather curl up quietly with a good book. If you 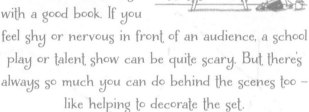 feel shy or nervous in front of an audience, a school play or talent show can be quite scary. But there's always so much you can do behind the scenes too – like helping to decorate the set.

Costume design can be one of the most fun parts about putting on a show! Why not have a go at designing an amazing costume opposite, for you or your friends to wear? Be as creative as you can. Here are some ideas for things you can use:

Feathers ★ Silk ribbons ★ A top hat
Real or fake flowers ★ Face paints ★ Pipe cleaners
★ Colourful leggings ★ A pair of fairy wings
★ A feather boa ★ Temporary tattoos
Bright red lipstick ★ Glittery make-up

nathing realy

DESIGN YOUR POSTER!

If you're planning a show, bright posters are the best
way to invite people along! Have a go at designing
yours here. Use your most colourful pencils or
felt tips. You could even add glitter!

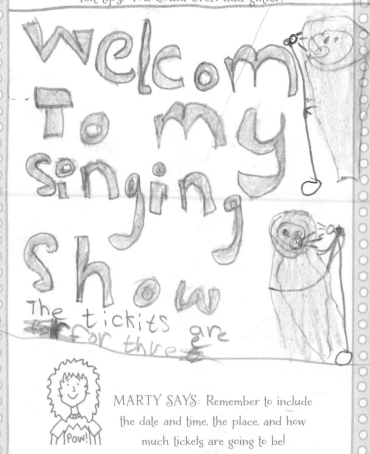

MARTY SAYS: Remember to include
the date and time, the place, and how
much tickets are going to be!

AUTOGRAPHS!

Do you think you or any of your friends will be truly famous one day? Ask everyone in your show to write their signatures on this page. In ten or twenty years, you'll be able to look at it and remember who took part. And if anyone has become a superstar, you'll have their autograph!

WRITE YOUR OWN PLAY!

You might decide to put on a famous play, but it would be fun to write your own too! Scribble down your ideas here. Who are your main characters, and what happens to them?

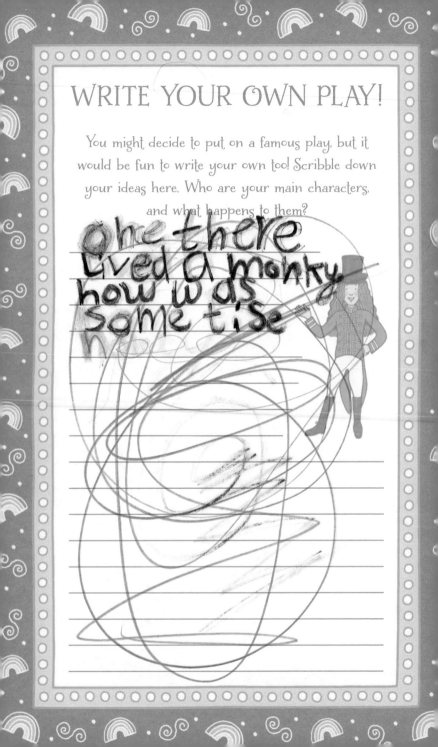

one there
Lived a monky
how was
some tise

☆ TRACY BEAKER'S ☆ TOTALLY TERRIFIC TALENT QUIZ! ☆

Test yourself and your friends and see who knows Jacqueline's books the best!

1. In *Little Darlings*, Destiny inherited her lovely singing voice from her pop-star dad. What is his name?

2. In *Starring Tracy Beaker*, Tracy is given the part of Ebenezer Scrooge. What famous story is her class performing?

3. *Hetty Feather* was adapted into a play recently. Which other Jacqueline Wilson book, starring twin sisters, has also been turned into a play?

4. Which Jacqueline Wilson character loves telling jokes and wants to be a famous comedienne?

5. In *Vicky Angel*, Jade loves acting and joins the Drama Club. She joins another club too – one she doesn't like anywhere near as much! What is it?

6. Tracy Beaker's adventures were turned into a television programme. Which actress played Tracy?

7. In *The Illustrated Mum*, one of the characters loves an old band called Emerald City – who is it?

8. Ellen-Jane Potts is a character who takes on a stage name when she becomes an acrobat. What is this stage name?

9. In *Double Act*, Ruby and Garnet audition to play a famous pair of twins on television: the Twins at St Clare's. Which author wrote those books?

10. Which character gets a job sewing costumes for the performers in the circus?

You'll find the answers at the back of this diary!

JANUARY

'I'd give anything to be a terrible show-off,' Peter said earnestly. 'Can't you show me how, Tracy? Is there a special trick?'

'It's just a natural gift, Peter,' I said. 'I was born showing off. I shot out of my mum and said, "Hi, folks!" to the doctor and the nurse, and then I turned a somersault, stood on my tiny feet and did a little tap dance on the delivery table.' *STARRING TRACY BEAKER*

Monday 29 December

Tuesday 30 December

Wednesday 31 December

Thursday 1 January

Friday 2 January

Saturday 3 January

Sunday 4 January

Monday 5 January

Tuesday 6 January

Wednesday 7 January

Thursday 8 January

Friday 9 January

Saturday 10 January

Sunday 11 January

Notes

Monday 12 January

Tuesday 13 January

Wednesday 14 January

Thursday 15 January

Friday 16 January

Saturday 17 January

Sunday 18 January

Notes

Monday 19 January

_____

Tuesday 20 January

_____

Wednesday 21 January

_____

Thursday 22 January

Friday 23 January

Saturday 24 January

Sunday 25 January

Notes

Monday 26 January

Tuesday 27 January

Wednesday 28 January

Thursday 29 January

Friday 30 January

Saturday 31 January

Sunday 1 February

Notes

FEBRUARY

Honestly, Garnet, give over jogging me. (She can be a bit stupid and shy at times. She doesn't think we'll ever make it as flashy film stars, but I keep telling her all we need is CONFIDENCE. She keeps going on at me now, saying she doesn't want to be a star. Well, that's mad. She can't mean it. Who on earth wouldn't want to show off all day in front of the camera and go to posh parties every night with all the other stars?)
DOUBLE ACT

Monday 2 February

Tuesday 3 February

Wednesday 4 February

Thursday 5 February

Friday 6 February

Saturday 7 February

Sunday 8 February

Monday 9 February

Tuesday 10 February

Wednesday 11 February

Thursday 12 February

Friday 13 February

Saturday 14 February

Sunday 15 February

Notes

Monday 16 February

Tuesday 17 February

Wednesday 18 February

Thursday 19 February

Friday 20 February

Saturday 21 February

Sunday 22 February

Notes

Monday 23 February

Tuesday 24 February

Wednesday 25 February

Thursday 26 February

Friday 27 February

Saturday 28 February

Sunday 1 March

Notes

MARCH

Ever since I was little I've wanted to be an actress. I know it's mad. I'm not anyone special. No-one from our estate ever gets to do anything glamorous or famous, and anyway, even the richest, prettiest, most talented kids can't make a living out of acting. But I just want to act so much. *VICKY ANGEL*

Monday 2 March	Sunday 1 March
Mollie	Jesse

Tuesday 3 March

Wednesday 4 March

Thursday 5 March

Friday 6 March

Saturday 7 March

Tamzin

Sunday 8 March

Monday 9 March

Tuesday 10 March

Wednesday 11 March

Thursday 12 March

Friday 13 March

_____

Saturday 14 March

_____

Sunday 15 March

_____

Notes

Monday 16 March

Tuesday 17 March

Wednesday 18 March

Thursday 19 March

Friday 20 March

Saturday 21 March

Sunday 22 March

Notes

Monday 23 March

Tuesday 24 March

Wednesday 25 March

Thursday 26 March

Friday 27 March

_____

Saturday 28 March

Sunday 29 March

_____

Notes

APRIL

He did a little tap dance on the grass, his feet flashing. He landed elegantly with a 'Ta-da!', his arms held high. 'Bravo!' I said, and clapped him. 'You're good at it, Bertie, really good.'
SAPPHIRE BATTERSEA

Monday 30 March

Tuesday 31 March

Wednesday 1 April

Thursday 2 April

_____

Friday 3 April

_____

Saturday 4 April

_____

Sunday 5 April

Monday 6 April

Tuesday 7 April

Wednesday 8 April

Thursday 9 April

Friday 10 April

Saturday 11 April

Sunday 12 April

Notes

Monday 13 April

Tuesday 14 April

Wednesday 15 April

Thursday 16 April

Friday 17 April

_____

Saturday 18 April

_____

Sunday 19 April

_____

Notes

Monday 20 April

Tuesday 21 April

Wednesday 22 April

Thursday 23 April

Friday 24 April

Saturday 25 April

Sunday 26 April

Notes

Monday 27 April

Tuesday 28 April

Wednesday 29 April

Thursday 30 April

MAY

As soon as I've sung, 'You are my Destiny,' I'm there in the song, on a different planet, and I'm feeling the words, the soar and sweep of them making the hairs stand up on my arms, and I carry on to the last beautiful long note, letting it all out.
LITTLE DARLINGS

Friday 1 May

Saturday 2 May

Sunday 3 May

Monday 4 May

Tuesday 5 May

Wednesday 6 May

Thursday 7 May

Friday 8 May

Saturday 9 May

Sunday 10 May

Notes

Monday 11 May

___

Tuesday 12 May

___

Wednesday 13 May

___

Thursday 14 May

Friday 15 May

_____

Saturday 16 May

_____

Sunday 17 May

_____

Notes

Monday 18 May

Tuesday 19 May

Wednesday 20 May

Thursday 21 May

Friday 22 May

Carol Singer

Victorian Gentleman

Victorian Lady

Saturday 23 May

Sunday 24 May

Notes

Monday 25 May

Tuesday 26 May

Wednesday 27 May

Thursday 28 May

Friday 29 May

_____

Saturday 30 May

_____

Sunday 31 May

_____

Notes

JUNE

We did this special dance over and over until we all knew it backwards (though Bella still faced backwards if you didn't watch her). Then we performed it like a real girl group to Amy's mum and her dad and her nan and they all clapped and clapped and said we were great.
SLEEPOVERS

Monday 1 June

Tuesday 2 June

Wednesday 3 June

Thursday 4 June

Friday 5 June

Saturday 6 June

Sunday 7 June

Monday 8 June

Tuesday 9 June

Wednesday 10 June

Thursday 11 June

Friday 12 June

Saturday 13 June

Sunday 14 June

Notes

Marley's Ghost

Spirit of Christmas Yet to Come

Spirit of Christmas Present

Monday 15 June

Tuesday 16 June

Wednesday 17 June

Thursday 18 June

Friday 19 June

Saturday 20 June

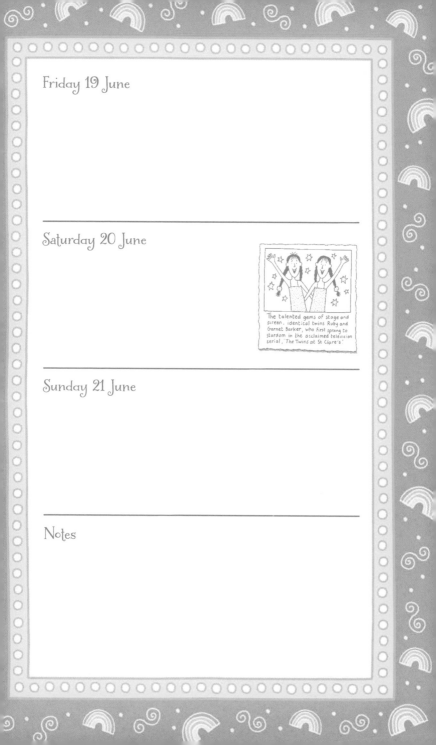

The talented gems of stage and screen, identical twins Ruby and Garnet Barker, who first sprang to stardom in the acclaimed television serial, 'The Twins at St Clare's'

Sunday 21 June

Notes

Monday 22 June

Tuesday 23 June

Wednesday 24 June

Thursday 25 June

Friday 26 June

Saturday 27 June

Sunday 28 June

Notes

JULY

Ruby grabbed me by the hand and hissed 'Twin-grin' and marched us into the middle of the stage. 'Hi, twins,' said this woman with short hair and a smock. 'Hi there,' said Ruby, imitating her voice, trying to sound all cool and casual, though I could see little beads of sweat on her forehead. She nudged me, and I squeaked 'Hi' too.
DOUBLE ACT

Monday 29 June

Tuesday 30 June

Wednesday 1 July

Thursday 2 July

Friday 3 July

Saturday 4 July

Sunday 5 July

Monday 6 July

Tuesday 7 July

Wednesday 8 July

Thursday 9 July

Friday 10 July

_____

Saturday 11 July

_____

Sunday 12 July

_____

Notes

Monday 13 July

Tuesday 14 July

Wednesday 15 July

Thursday 16 July

Friday 17 July

Saturday 18 July

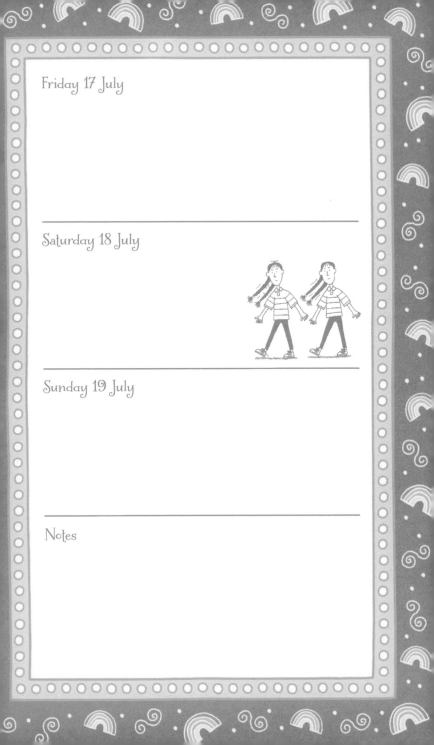

Sunday 19 July

Notes

Monday 20 July

Tuesday 21 July

Wednesday 22 July

Thursday 23 July

Friday 24 July

_____

Saturday 25 July

_____

Sunday 26 July

_____

Notes

Monday 27 July

_____

Tuesday 28 July

_____

Wednesday 29 July

_____

Thursday 30 July

Friday 31 July

Saturday 1 August

Sunday 2 August

Notes

AUGUST

I made up this story to myself that I was a famous
comedienne and I'd just done this amazingly
funny routine on stage and everyone had laughed
and laughed and then they'd clapped and clapped and
begged for an encore and showered me with roses . . .
THE BED AND BREAKFAST STAR

Monday 3 August

Tuesday 4 August

Wednesday 5 August

Thursday 6 August

Friday 7 August

Saturday 8 August

Sunday 9 August

Monday 10 August

Tuesday 11 August

Wednesday 12 August

Thursday 13 August

Friday 14 August

Saturday 15 August

Sunday 16 August

Notes

Monday 17 August

Tuesday 18 August

Wednesday 19 August

Thursday 20 August

Friday 21 August

Saturday 22 August

Sunday 23 August

Notes

Monday 24 August

Tuesday 25 August

Wednesday 26 August

Thursday 27 August

Friday 28 August

Saturday 29 August

Sunday 30 August

Notes

SEPTEMBER

'As I've got the biggest part you'd better give me a copy of the play straight away, Miss Simpkins, so I can get to be word perfect. In fact, maybe I ought to be excused all the boring lessons like literacy and maths just so I can concentrate on learning my part.'
STARRING TRACY BEAKER

Monday 31 August

Tuesday 1 September

Wednesday 2 September

Thursday 3 September

_____

Friday 4 September

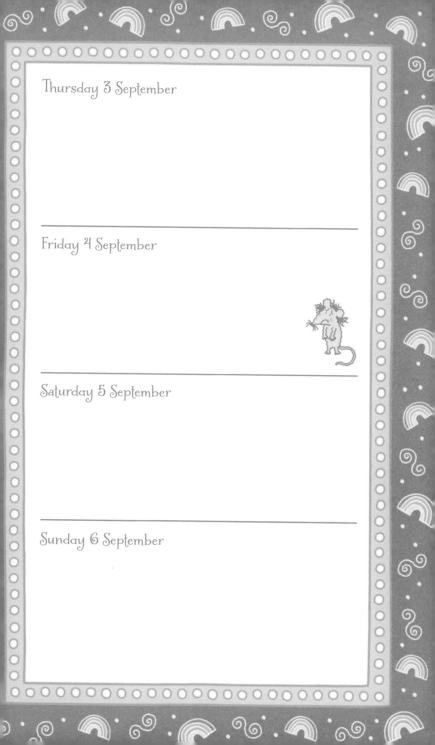

_____

Saturday 5 September

_____

Sunday 6 September

Monday 7 September

Sofia

Tuesday 8 September

Wednesday 9 September

Thursday 10 September

Friday 11 September

Saturday 12 September

Sunday 13 September

Notes

Monday 14 September

Tuesday 15 September

Wednesday 16 September

Thursday 17 September

Friday 18 September

_____

Saturday 19 September

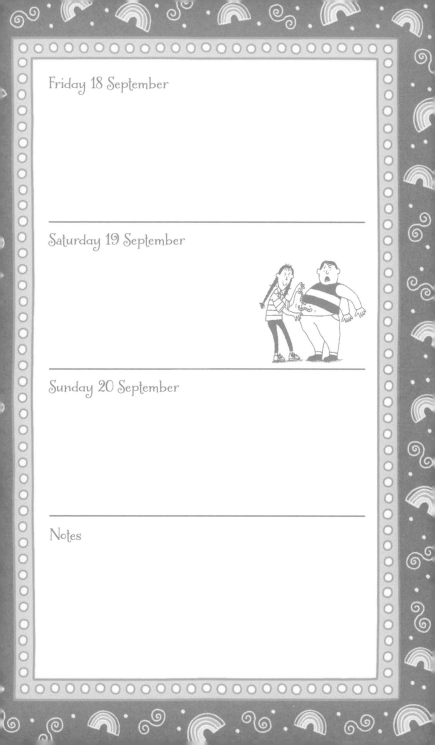

_____

Sunday 20 September

_____

Notes

Monday 21 September

Tuesday 22 September

Wednesday 23 September

Thursday 24 September

Friday 25 September

Saturday 26 September

Sunday 27 September

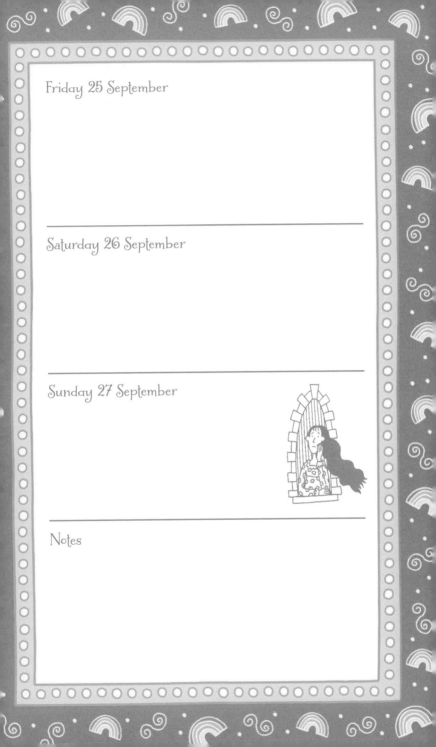

Notes

Monday 28 September

Tuesday 29 September

Wednesday 30 September

Thursday 1 October

OCTOBER

I could not walk in my costume. I could not even stand. I lay down gingerly on the dirty tarpaulin. I let my hair down and combed it vigorously, trying to look as fetching as possible. Then I called out: 'Roll up, roll up, come and see the new attraction at Mr Clarendon's Seaside Curiosities! Marvel at Emerald, the Amazing Pocket-Sized Mermaid.'
SAPPHIRE BATTERSEA

Friday 2 October

Saturday 3 October

Sunday 4 October

Monday 5 October

Tuesday 6 October

Wednesday 7 October

Thursday 8 October

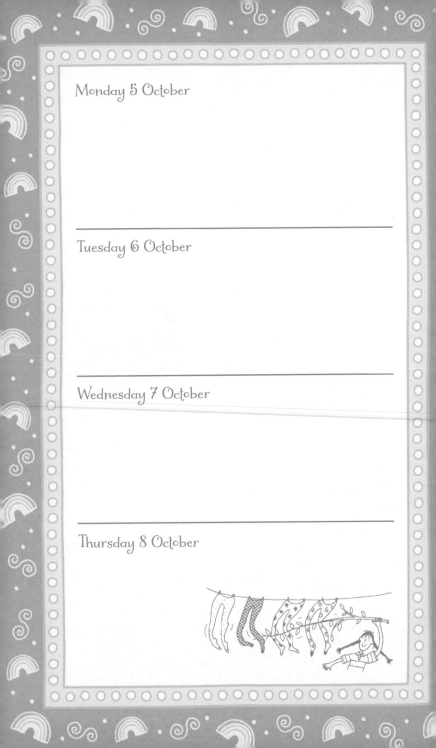

Friday 9 October

Saturday 10 October

Sunday 11 October

Notes

Monday 12 October

Tuesday 13 October

Wednesday 14 October

Thursday 15 October

Friday 16 October

Saturday 17 October

Sunday 18 October

Notes

Monday 19 October

Tuesday 20 October

Wednesday 21 October

Thursday 22 October

Friday 23 October

Saturday 24 October

Sunday 25 October

Notes

Monday 26 October

Tuesday 27 October

Wednesday 28 October

Thursday 29 October

Friday 30 October

Saturday 31 October

Sunday 1 November

Notes

NOVEMBER

Miss Gilmore, who's head of English and Drama, had us all in Toad of Toad Hall when we were in Year Seven. I so wanted to be Toad, but Miss Gilmore chose Fatboy Sam. Typecasting. Though he was good. Very good. But I have this mad, totally secret idea that I could have been better.
VICKY ANGEL

Monday 2 November

Tuesday 3 November

Wednesday 4 November

Thursday 5 November

Friday 6 November

Saturday 7 November

Sunday 8 November

Monday 9 November

Tuesday 10 November

Wednesday 11 November

Thursday 12 November

Friday 13 November

Saturday 14 November

Sunday 15 November

Notes

Monday 16 November

Tuesday 17 November

Wednesday 18 November

Thursday 19 November

Friday 20 November

Saturday 21 November

Sunday 22 November

Notes

Monday 23 November

~~Rebecca~~ kate
my sister

Tuesday 24 November

Wednesday 25 November

Thursday 26 November

Friday 27 November

Saturday 28 November

Sunday 29 November

Mia My sister

Notes

DECEMBER

I am soon going to be acclaimed as a brilliant child
star. I have the STAR part in a major production
this Christmas. Truly. I am in our school's play
of *A Christmas Carol.*
STARRING TRACY BEAKER

Monday 30 November

~~Joney MY~~
~~bobruther~~

Tuesday 1 December

~~bailey but~~
~~bailey my brother~~

LITTLE DARLINGS

Wednesday 2 December

bailey

Thursday 3 December

Friday 4 December

Saturday 5 December

Sunday 6 December

Monday 7 December

Tuesday 8 December

Wednesday 9 December

Thursday 10 December

Friday 11 December

Saturday 12 December

Sunday 13 December

Notes

Monday 14 December

boby My ~~bro brt~~
brother

_____

Tuesday 15 December

_____

Wednesday 16 December

_____

Thursday 17 December

Friday 18 December

Saturday 19 December

Sunday 20 December

Notes

Monday 21 December

_____

Tuesday 22 December

_____

Wednesday 23 December

_____

Thursday 24 December

Friday 25 December

Saturday 26 December

Sunday 27 December

Notes

Monday 28 December

Tuesday 29 December

Wednesday 30 December

Thursday 31 December

Friday 1 January

_____

Saturday 2 January

_____

Sunday 3 January

_____

Notes

REVIEWS!

Who came to watch your show? Ask your audience to write reviews on the next few pages. They might even want to give you five stars!

George

Anhgan

Lewiss

~~Danny~~

~~have been~~
~~been very~~
~~daytight and~~
~~I'm very~~
~~scer of it.~~

Walk
My dog
every

SUNDAy

Sunday
Sunday

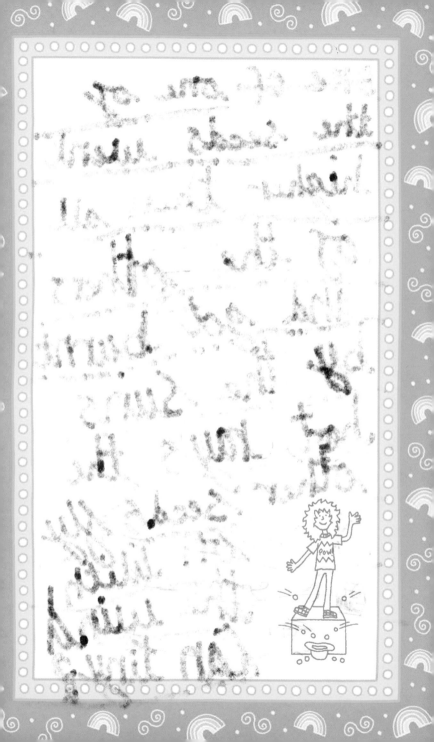

~~one of~~ one of
the seeds went
higher then all
of the others
and got burnt
by the suns
hot rays the
other seeds fly
on with
the wind
can tiny?

CHECK OUT
JACQUELINE WILSON'S
OFFICIAL WEBSITE!

There's a whole Jacqueline Wilson town to explore! You can generate your own special username, customise your online bedroom, test your knowledge of Jacqueline's books with fun quizzes and puzzles, and upload book reviews. There's lots of fun stuff to discover, including competitions, book trailers, and Jacqueline's scrapbook. And if you love writing, visit the special storytelling area!

Plus, you can hear the latest news from Jacqueline in her monthly diary, find out whether she's doing events near you, read her fan-mail replies, and chat to other fans on the message boards!

Have you seen this other
gorgeous stationery?

THE JACQUELINE WILSON DIARY 2015
A DOUBLEDAY BOOK 978 0 857 53198 8

Published in Great Britain by Doubleday,
an imprint of Random House Children's Publishers UK.
A Random House Group Company

This edition published 2014

1 3 5 7 9 10 8 6 4 2

Copyright © Jacqueline Wilson, 2007, 2014
Illustrations copyright © Nick Sharratt, 2007, 2014
Illustrations copyright © Sue Heap, 2007, 2014

The Random House Group Limited supports the Forest Stewardship Council® (FSC®),
the leading international forest-certification organisation. Our books carrying the FSC label
are printed on FSC®-certified paper. FSC is the only forest-certification scheme supported
by the leading environmental organisations, including Greenpeace. Our paper procurement
policy can be found at www.randomhouse.co.uk/environment.

Set in Liam

RANDOM HOUSE CHILDREN'S PUBLISHERS UK
61–63 Uxbridge Road, London W5 5SA

www.randomhousechildren.co.uk
www.totallyrandombooks.co.uk
www.randomhouse.co.uk

Addresses for companies within The Random House Group Limited can be found at:
www.randomhouse.co.uk/offices.htm

THE RANDOM HOUSE GROUP Limited Reg. No. 954009

A CIP catalogue record for this book is available from the British Library.

Printed and bound in China

PUZZLE ANSWERS

1. Danny Kilman
2. A Christmas Carol
3. Double Act
4. Elsa
5. Running Club
6. Dani Harmer
7. Marigold
8. Diamond
9. Enid Blyton
10. Hetty Feather

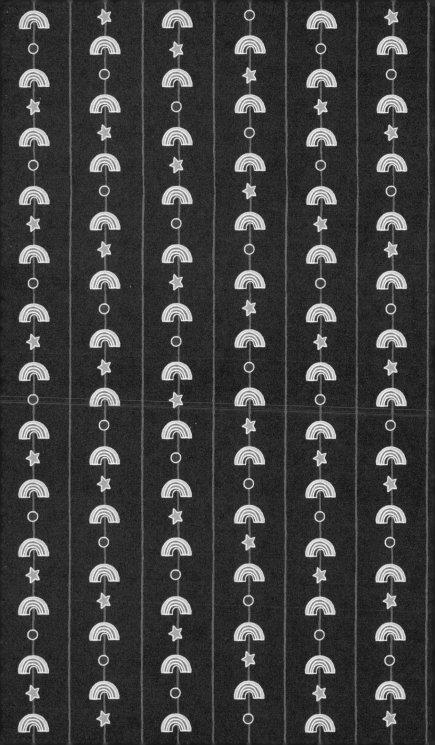